FART
COLORING BOOK

Join our mailing list to be among

the first to find out about special offers,

discounts and our new releases!

Sign up at:
www.adultcoloringworld.net

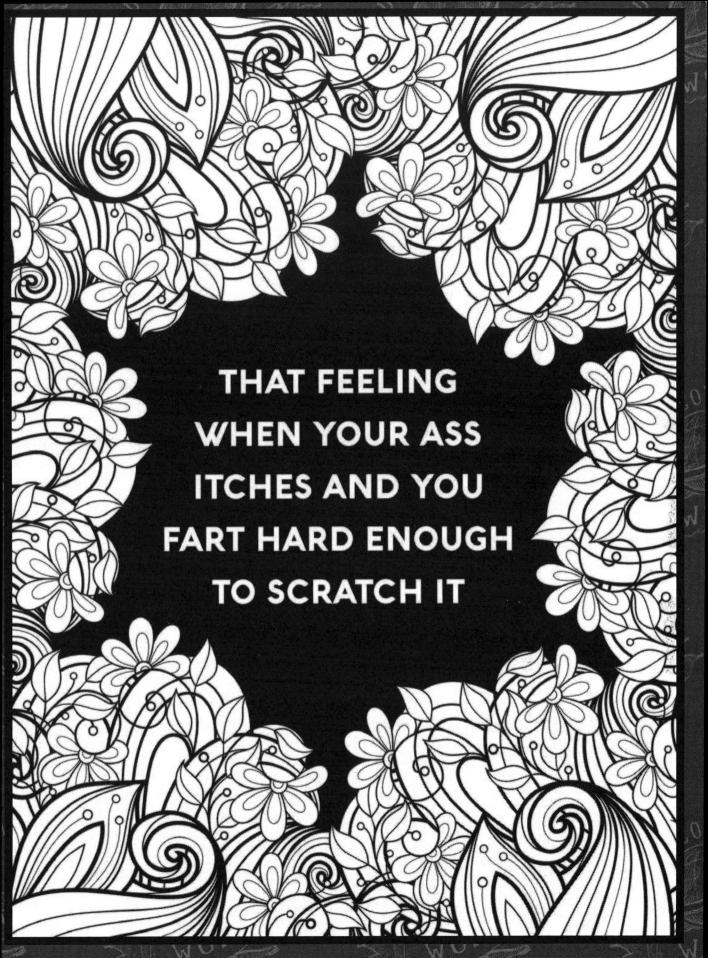

THAT FEELING
WHEN YOUR ASS
ITCHES AND YOU
FART HARD ENOUGH
TO SCRATCH IT

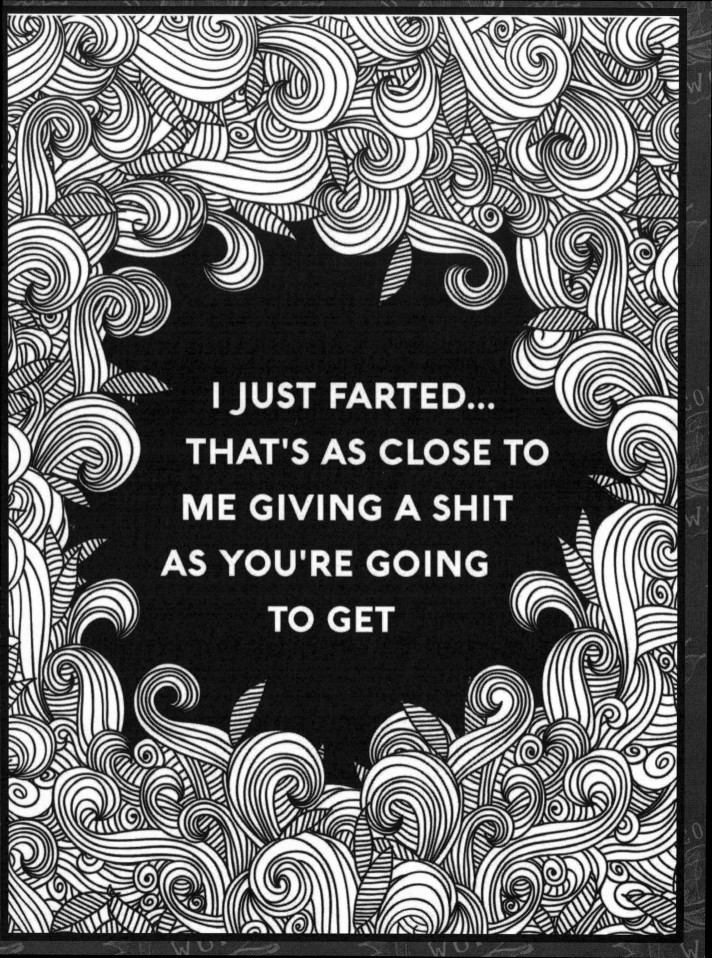

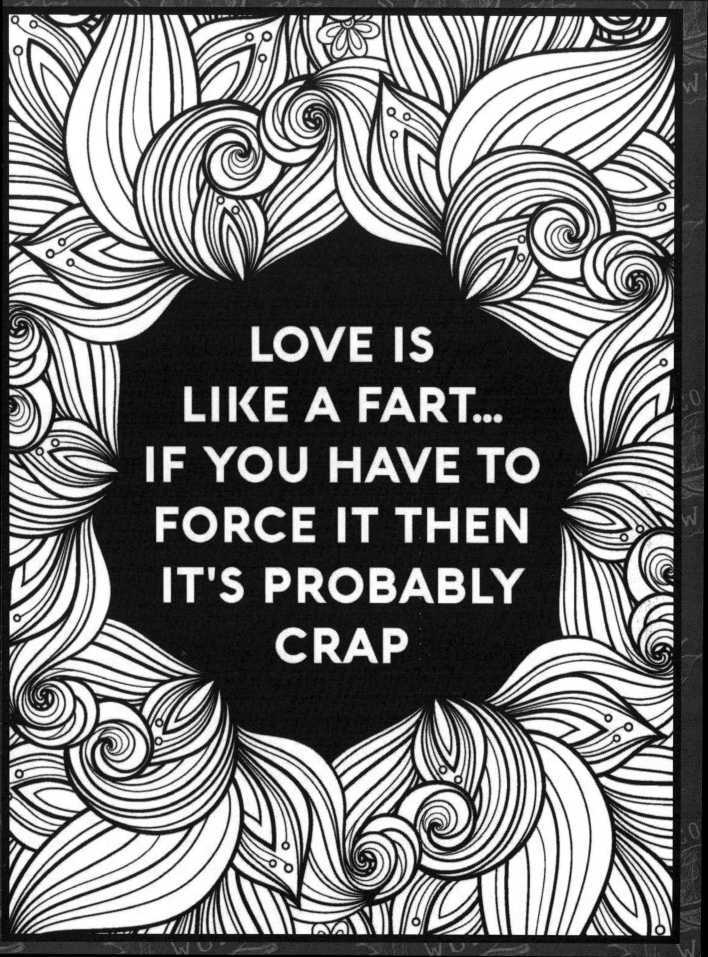

AIR BUFFET:
LIKE AN AIR BISCUIT
BUT IT LINGERS AND
CAN BE REVISITED
MANY TIMES

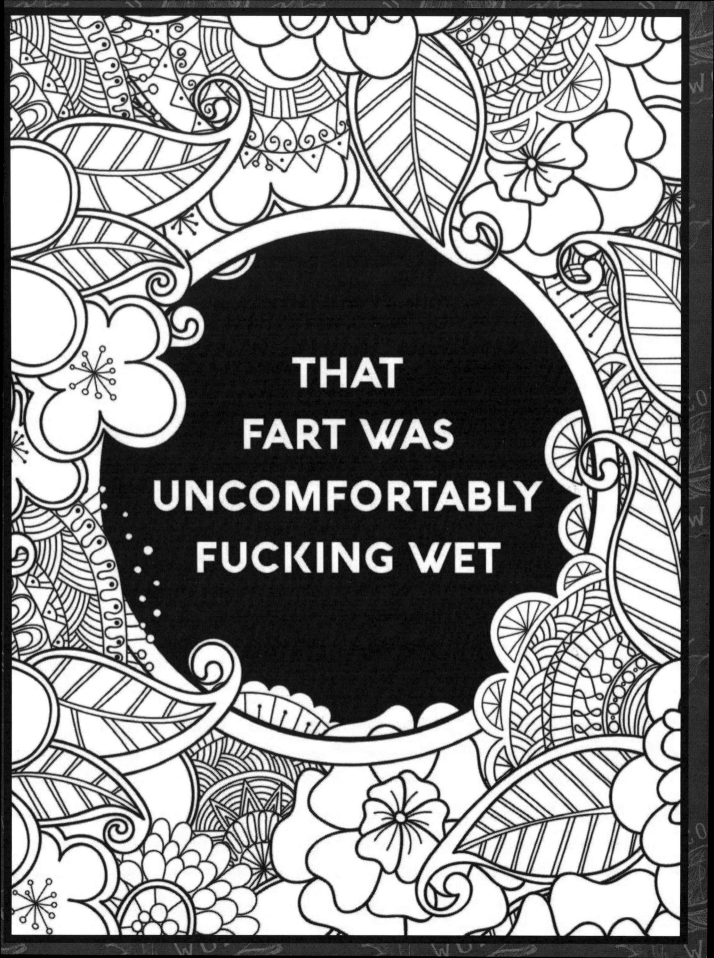

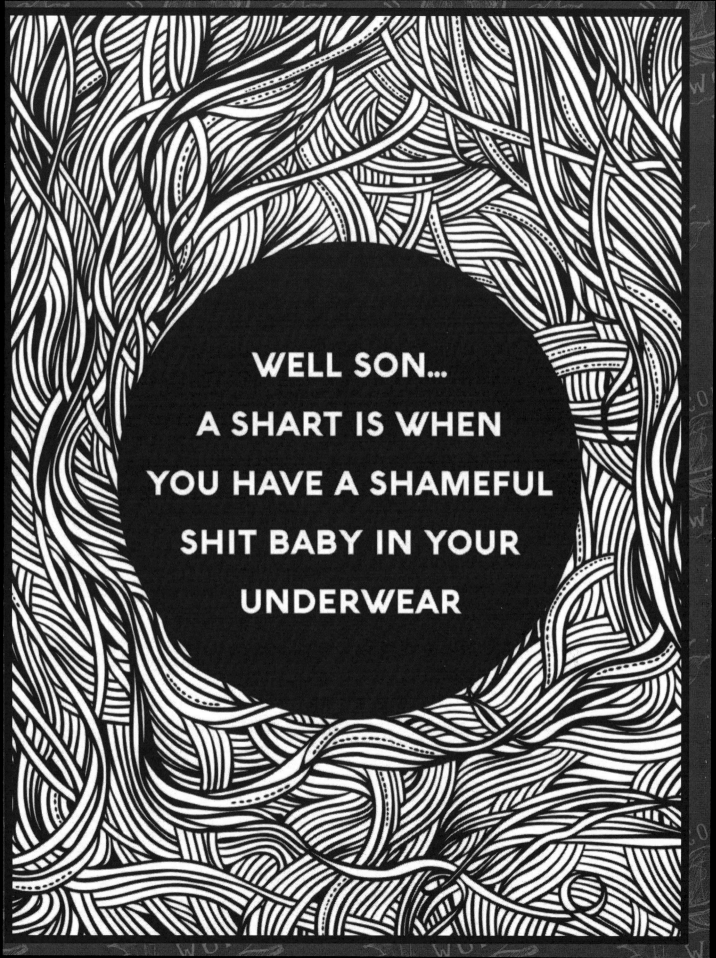

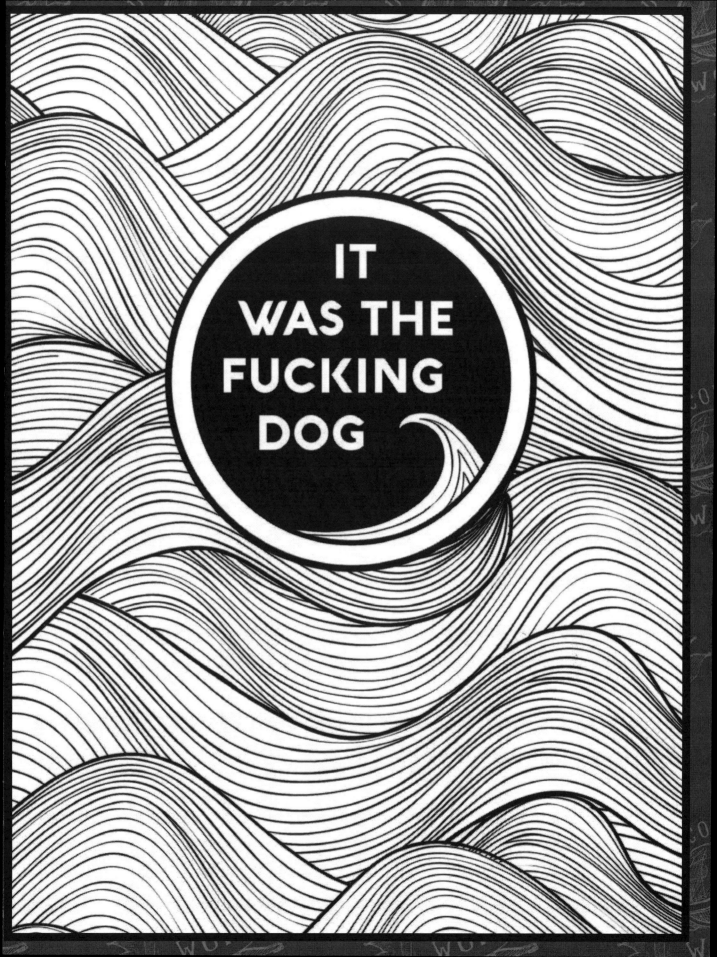

I CAN
FEEL THAT FART...
RUNNING DOWN
THE BACK OF
MY FUCKING
KNEE

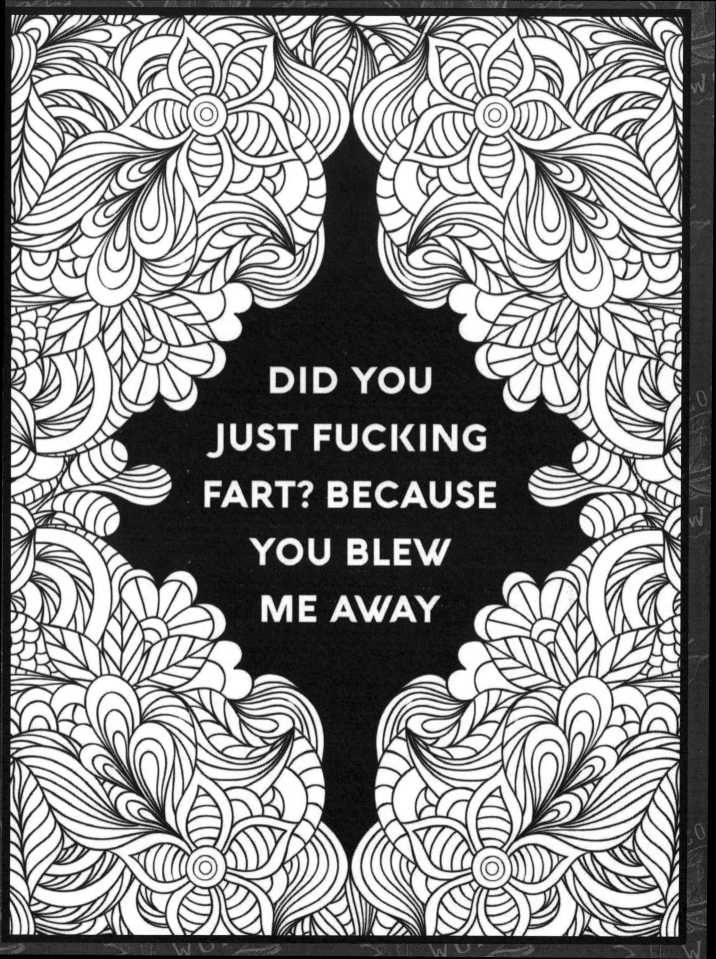

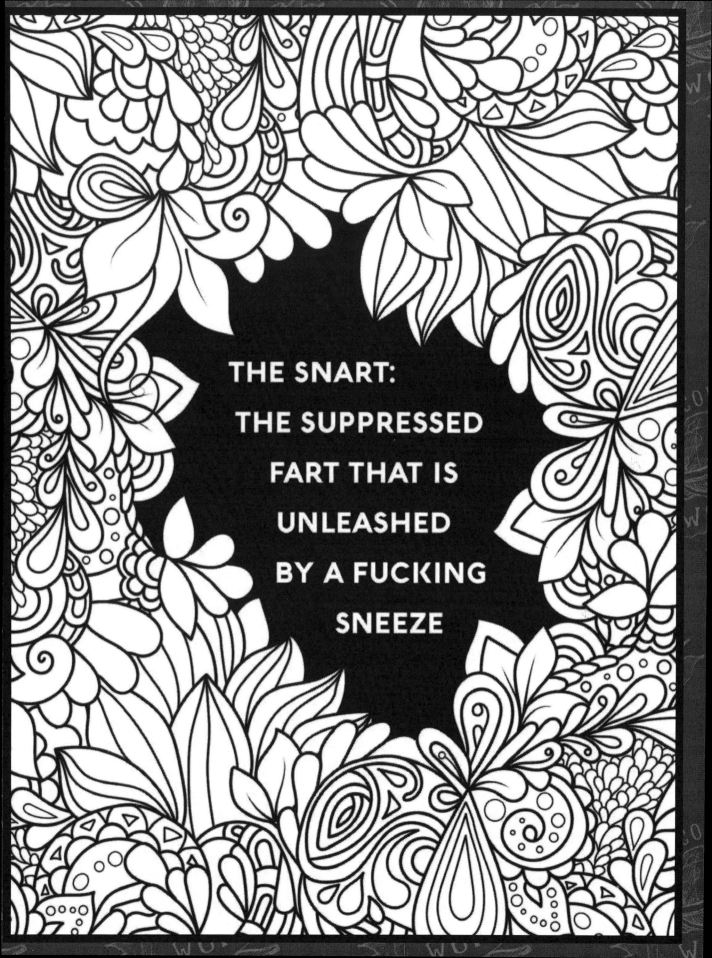

THE SNART:
THE SUPPRESSED
FART THAT IS
UNLEASHED
BY A FUCKING
SNEEZE

THE
BREATHER:
A FUCKING HUGE
EXHALE OF GAS
MUCH LIKE
A SIGH

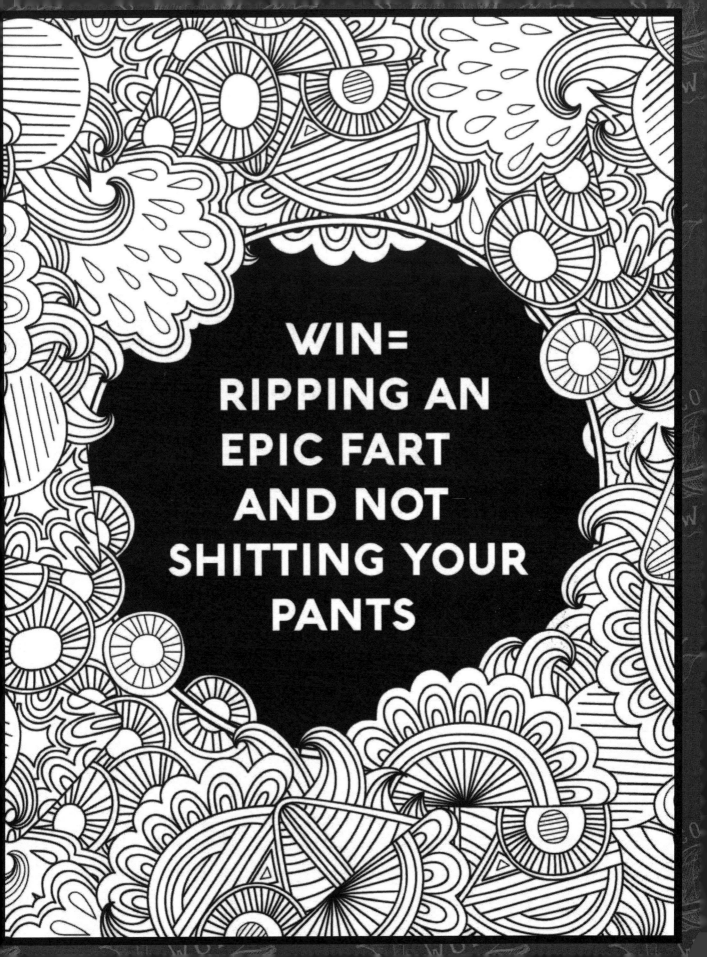

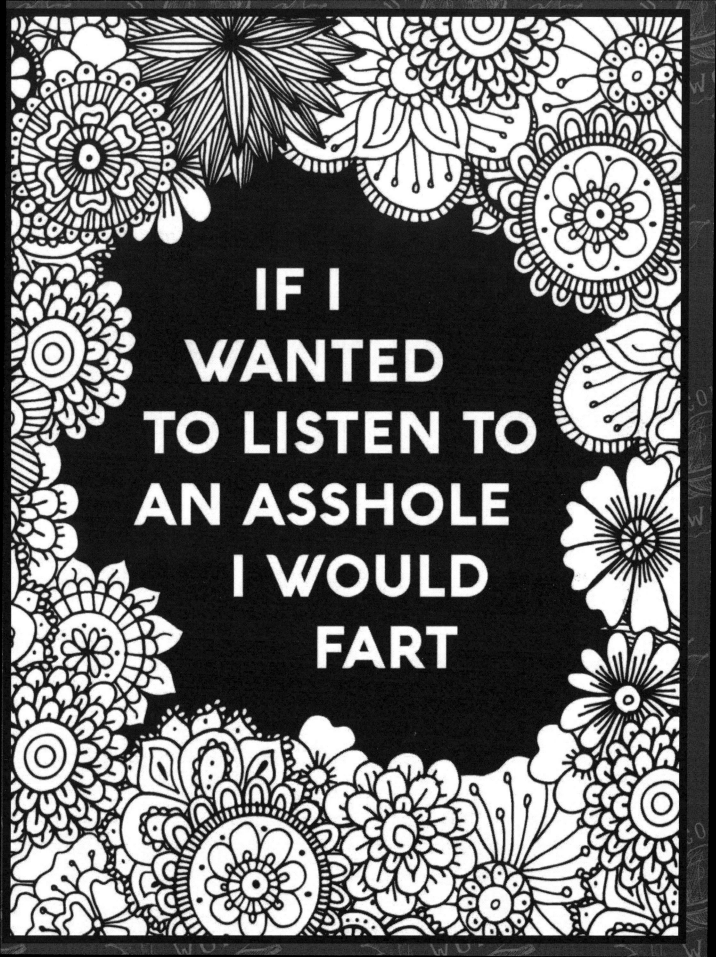

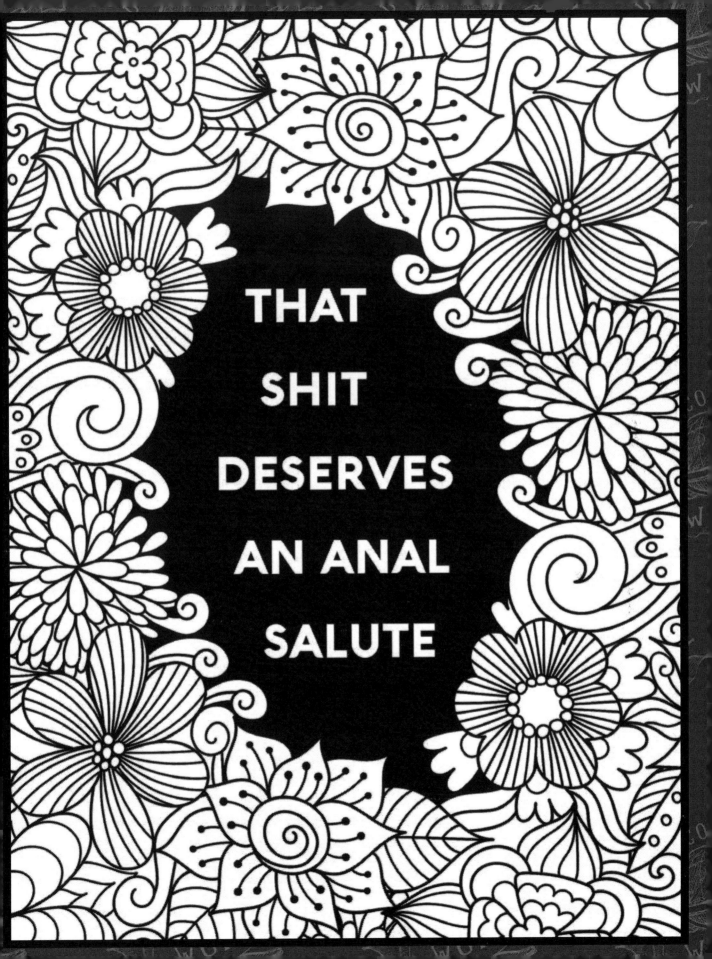

MY GOAL
IN LIFE IS TO
FART LOUD
ENOUGH TO
TRIGGER A CAR
ALARM

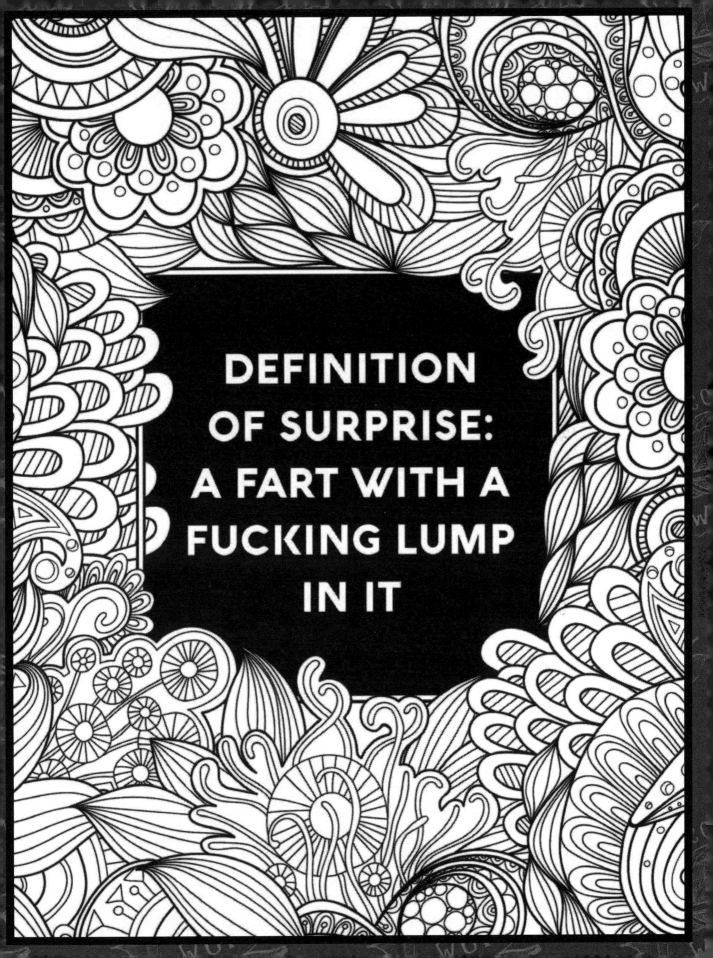

DEFINITION OF SURPRISE: A FART WITH A FUCKING LUMP IN IT

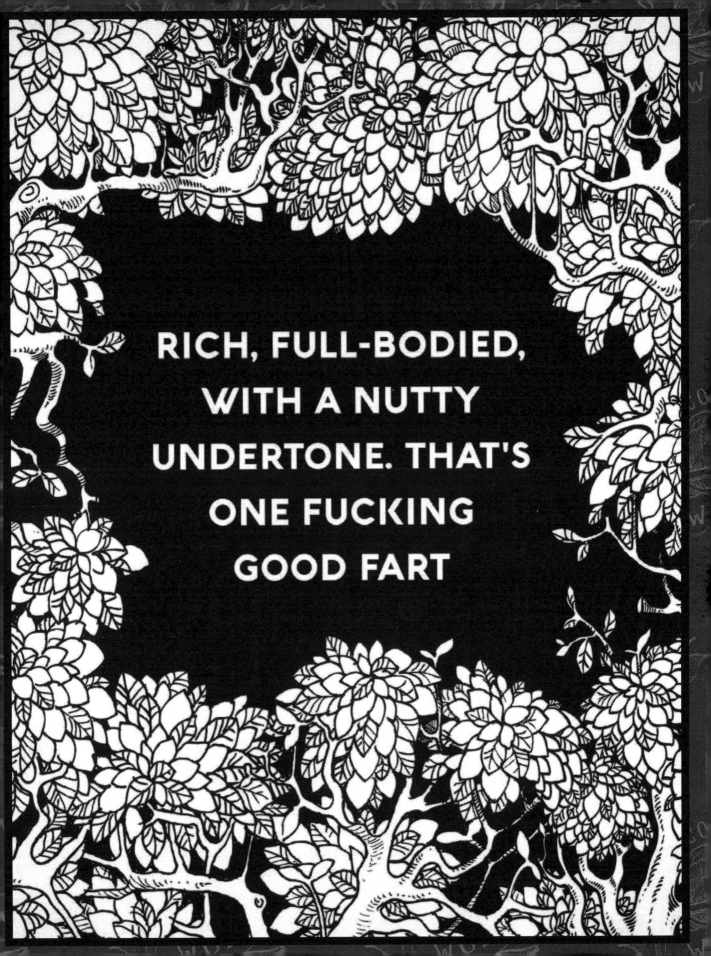

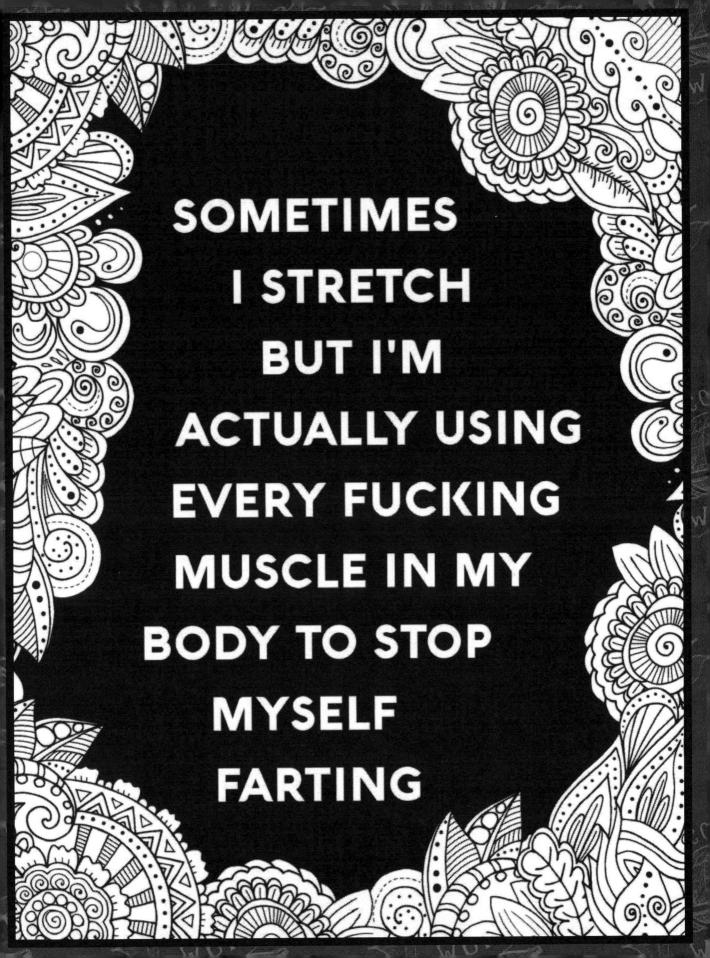

SOMETIMES I STRETCH BUT I'M ACTUALLY USING EVERY FUCKING MUSCLE IN MY BODY TO STOP MYSELF FARTING

TIME TO ANSWER THE CALL OF THE WILD FUCKING BURRITO

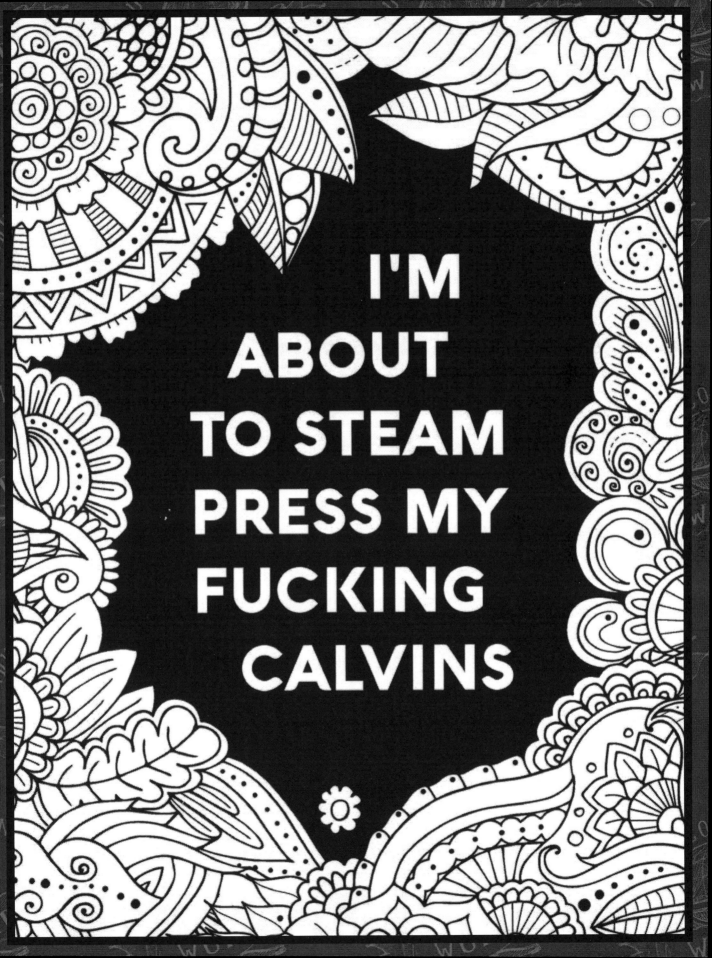

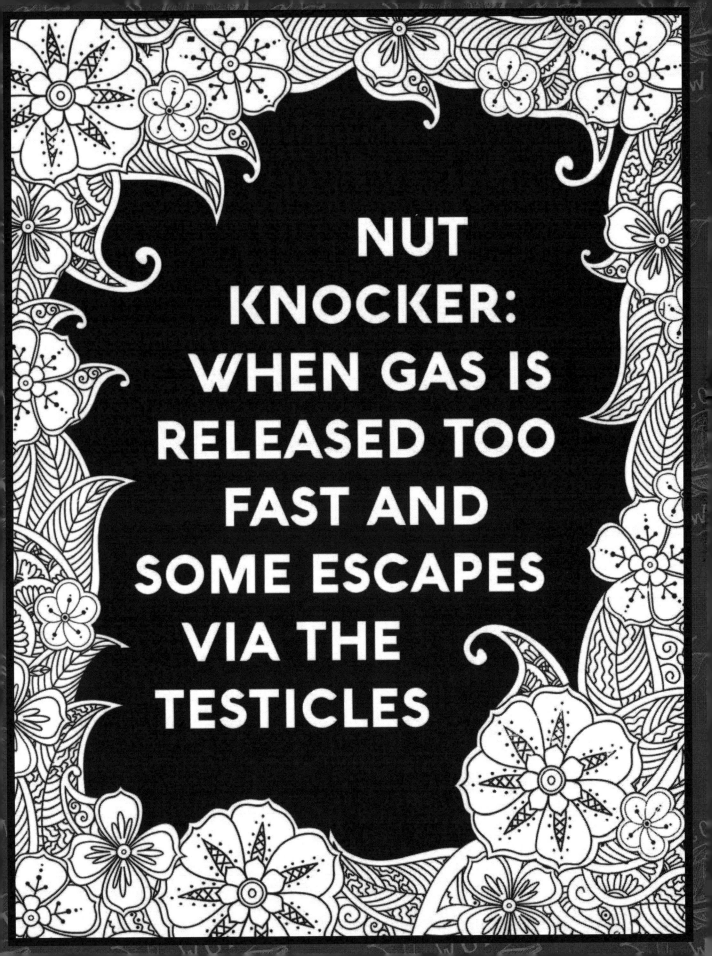

COLOR TEST
PAGE

COLOR TEST
PAGE

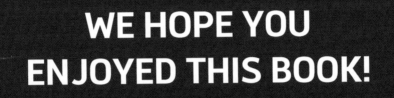

WE HOPE YOU ENJOYED THIS BOOK!

TO VIEW OUR HUGE RANGE OF ADULT COLORING BOOKS, VISIT OUR WEBSITE TODAY:

ADULTCOLORINGWORLD.NET

Made in the USA
San Bernardino, CA
22 January 2018